Design Directory

Citrus Salad
Page 2

Strawberry Shortcake
Page 3

Fresh Persimmon
Page 4

Garden Rows
Page 5

Cherry Pie
Page 6

Key Lime Pie
Page 7

Pistachio Nut Surprise
Page 8

Plum Jelly
Page 9

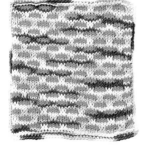

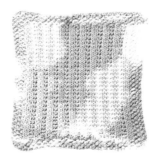

Tossed Salad
Page 10

Blueberry Muffins
Page 11

Blueberries & Cream
Page 12

Blue Ribbon Pastry
Page 13

Skill Level

 EASY

Finished Size

Approx 10 inches square

Materials

• Lily Sugar 'n Cream medium weight cotton yarn (120 yds/71g per ball): 1 ball each ivory #00007 (A) and hot green #01712 (B)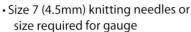
• Size 7 (4.5mm) knitting needles or size required for gauge
• Size 6/G (4mm) crochet hook

Gauge

17 sts = 4 inches/10cm in pat
To save time, take time to check gauge.

Pattern Notes

Slip all sts as if to purl.
Carry color not in use loosely along edge.

Instructions

With A, cast on 44 sts.
Knit 1 row.
Set up pat
Row 1 (RS): With A, knit.
Row 2: K1, purl to last st, k1.
Row 3: Knit.
Row 4: K1, purl to last st, k1.
Row 5: With B, k4, *sl 2 wyif, k2; rep from * across.
Row 6: K2, *sl 2 wyif, k2; rep from * to last 2 sts, k2.
Rows 7–10: Rep Rows 1–4.
Row 11: With B, k2, *sl 2 wyif, k2; rep from * to last 2 sts, k2.
Row 12: K4, *sl 2 wyif, k2; rep from * across.
[Rep rows 1–12] 4 times.
With A, knit 1 row.
Bind off.

Edging

Hold with RS facing and bound-off edge at top, with crochet hook, join B in upper right-hand corner, ch 1, 3 sc in same corner, sc evenly spaced around the outside of dishcloth, working 3 sc in each corner; join with sl st in first sc.
Finish off and weave in all ends. ●

Strawberry Shortcake

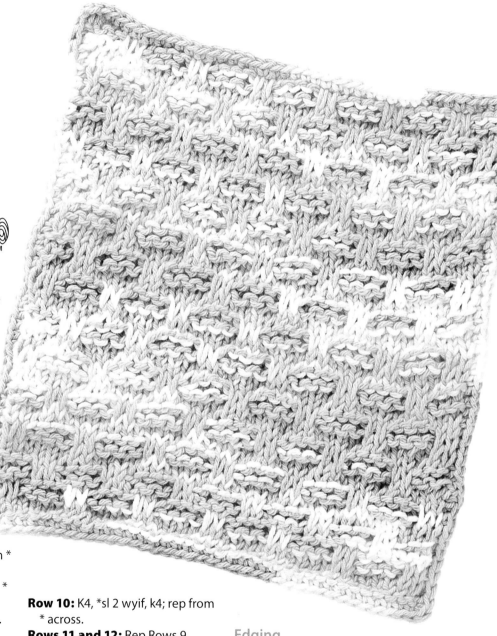

Skill Level

 EASY

Finished Size
Approx 9½ inches square

Materials
- Lily Sugar 'n Cream medium weight cotton yarn (95 yds/57g per ball): 1 ball rosewood #02510
- Size 7 (4.5mm) knitting needles or size needed to obtain gauge
- Size 6/G (4mm) crochet hook

Gauge
17 sts = 4 inches/10cm in pat
To save time, take time to check gauge.

Pattern Note
Slip all sts as if to purl.

Instructions

Cast on 40 sts.
Row 1 (RS): Knit.
Row 2: K1, purl to last st, k1.
Row 3: K1, *sl 2 wyib, k4; rep from * to last 3 sts, sl 2 wyib, k1.
Row 4: K1, *sl 2 wyif, k4; rep from * to last 3 sts, sl 2 wyif, k1.
Rows 5 and 6: Rep Rows 3 and 4.
Row 7: Knit.
Row 8: K1, purl to last st, k1.
Row 9: K4, *sl 2 wyib, k4; rep from * across.
Row 10: K4, *sl 2 wyif, k4; rep from * across.
Rows 11 and 12: Rep Rows 9 and 10.
[Rep Rows 1–12] 6 times.
Bind off, placing last st on crochet hook.

Edging
Ch 1, 3 sc in same corner, sc evenly spaced around the outside of the dishcloth, working 3 sc in each corner; join in first sc.
Finish off and weave in ends. ●

Fresh Persimmon

Skill Level

EASY

Finished Size
Approx 9½ inches square

Materials
- Peaches & Crème medium weight cotton yarn (122 yds/71g per ball): 1 ball brick red #96
- Size 7 (4.5mm) knitting needles or size needed to obtain gauge
- Size 6/G (4mm) crochet hook

Gauge
16 sts = 4 inches/10cm in pat
To save time, take time to check gauge.

Pattern Note
Slip all sts as if to purl.

Instructions

Cast on 38 sts.
Row 1 and all odd-numbered rows (WS): K1, purl to last st, k1.
Row 2 (RS): K1, *sl 3 wyif, k3; rep from * to last st, k1.
Row 4: K2, *sl 3 wyif, k3; rep from * across.
Row 6: K3, *sl 3 wyif, k3; rep from * to last 5 sts, sl 3 wyif, k2.
Row 8: K1, *k3, sl 3 wyif; rep from * to last st, k1.
Row 10: K1, sl 1 wyif, *k3, sl 3 wyif; rep from * to last 6 sts, k3, sl 2 wyif, k1.
Row 12: K1, sl 2 wyif, *k3, sl 3 wyif; rep from * to last 5 sts, k3, sl 1 wyif, k1.
[Rep Rows 1–12] 5 times.
Bind off, placing last st on crochet hook.

Edging
Ch 1, 3 sc in same corner, sc evenly spaced around the outside of dishcloth, working 3 sc in each corner; join with sl st in first sc.
Finish off and weave in ends. ●

American School of Needlework • Berne, Indiana 46711 • DRGnetwork.com

Garden Rows

Skill Level

 EASY

Finished Size
Approx 9½ inches square

Materials
- Lily Sugar 'n Cream medium weight cotton yarn (120 yds/71g per ball): 1 ball each hot blue #01742 (A), hot green #01712 (B), yellow #00010 (C) and white #00001 (D)
- Size 7 (4.5mm) knitting needles or size needed to obtain gauge
- Size 6/G (4mm) crochet hook

Gauge
18 sts = 4 inches/10cm in pat
To save time, take time to check gauge.

Pattern Notes
Slip all sts as if to purl.
Carry yarn not in use loosely along edge.

Instructions

With A, cast on 43 sts.
Row 1 (WS): K1, purl to last st, k1.
Row 2 (RS): With B, k2, *sl 1 wyib, k1; rep from * to last st, k1.
Row 3: K1, p1, *sl 1 wyif, p1; rep from * to last st, k1.
Row 4: With C, k1, *sl 1 wyib, k1; rep from * across.
Row 5: K1, purl to last st, k1.
Row 6: With D, k1, *sl 1 wyib, k3; rep from * to last 2 sts, sl 1 wyib, k1.
Row 7: K1, *sl 1 wyif, p3; rep from * to last 2 sts, sl 1 wyif, k1.
Row 8: With B, k2, *sl 3 wyib, k1; rep from * to last st, k1.
Row 9: K1, p2, *sl 1 wyif, p3; rep from * to last 4 sts, sl 1 wyif, p2, k1.
Row 10: With A, k1, *sl 1 wyib, k3; rep from * to last 2 sts, sl 1 wyib, k1.
[Rep Rows 1–10] 6 times.
Bind off.

Edging
Hold with RS facing and bound-off edge at top, with crochet hook, join C in upper right-hand corner. Ch 1, 3 sc in same corner, sc evenly spaced around the outside of dishcloth, working 3 sc in each corner; join with sl st in first sc.
Finish off and weave in all ends. ●

Cherry Pie

Skill Level

◼◼◻◻ EASY

Finished Size

Approx 10 inches square

Materials

- Lily Sugar 'n Cream medium weight cotton yarn (120 yds/71g per ball): 1 ball red #00095 (A)
- Peaches & Crème medium weight cotton yarn (122 yds/71g per ball): 1 ball ecru #4 (B)
- Size 7 (4.5mm) knitting needles or size needed to obtain gauge
- Size 6/G (4mm) crochet hook
- Tapestry needle

Gauge

22 sts = 4 inches/10cm in pat
To save time, take time to check gauge.

Pattern Notes

Slip all sts as if to purl.
When working with both A and B, carry yarn not in use loosely along edge.

Instructions

Pattern Strip

Make 2
With A, cast on 22 sts.
Knit 1 row.

Set up block pat
Row 1 (RS): Knit.
Row 2: Purl.
Row 3: K2, [p8, k2] twice.
Row 4: P2, [k8, p2] twice.
Row 5: K2, [p2, k4, p2, k2] twice.
Row 6: P2, [k2, p4, k2, p2] twice.
Rows 7–10: [Rep Rows 5 and 6] twice.
Rows 11 and 12: Rep Rows 3 and 4.
Rep Rows 1–12.
Knit 2 rows.
Set up check pat
Row 1 (RS): With B, knit.
Row 2: Purl.
Row 3: With A, k1, *sl 2 wyib, k2; rep from * to last 3 sts, k3.
Row 4: K1, *p2, sl 2 wyif; rep from * to last st, k1.
Row 5: With B, knit.
Row 6: Purl.
Row 7: With A, k3, *sl 2 wyib, k2; rep from * to last 3 sts, sl 2 wyib, k1.
Row 8: With A, k1, *sl 2 wyif, p2; rep from * to last 3 sts, p3.
[Rep rows 1–8] 4 times.
Bind off.

Finishing

Turn one pattern strip in the opposite direction and sew to the other strip.
Hold with RS facing, attach A in upper right-hand corner, ch 1, 3 sc in same sp, sc evenly spaced around the outside of the dishcloth, working 3 sc in each corner; join with sl st in first sc.
Finish off and weave in all ends. ●

 American School of Needlework • Berne, Indiana 46711 • DRGnetwork.com

Key Lime Pie

Skill Level

■■□□ *EASY*

Finished Size

Approx 9 inches square

Materials

- Lily Sugar 'n Cream medium weight cotton yarn (120 yds/71g per ball): 1 ball each hot green #01712 (A) and white #00001 (B)
- Size 7 (4.5mm) knitting needles, or size necessary to obtain gauge
- Size 6/G (4mm) crochet hook

Gauge

17 sts = 4 inches/10cm in pat st
To save time, take time to check gauge.

Pattern Notes

Slip all sts as if to purl.
Carry color not in use loosely along edge.

Instructions

Lower Border

With A, cast on 40 sts.
With A, knit 4 rows.
With B, purl 3 rows.
With A, knit 4 rows.

Body

Row 1 (RS): With B, knit.
Row 2: With B, knit.
Row 3: With A, k1, *sl 2 wyib, k2; rep from * to last 3 sts, sl 2 wyib, k1.
Row 4: With A, p1, *sl 2 wyif, p2; rep from * to last 3 sts, sl 2 wyif, p1.

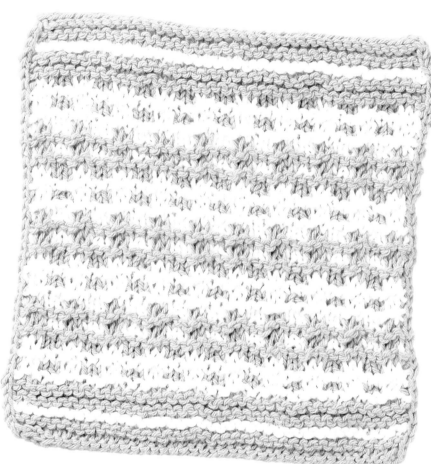

Row 5: With B, knit.
Row 6: With B, knit.
Row 7: With A, k1, *sl 2 wyib, k2; rep from * to last 3 sts, sl 2 wyib, k1.
Row 8: With A, p1, *sl 2 wyif, p2; rep from * to last 3 sts, sl 2 wyif, p1.
Row 9: With A, knit.
Row 10: With A, knit.
Row 11: With B, k1, *sl 2 wyib, k2; rep from * to last 3 sts, sl 2 wyib, k1.
Row 12: With B, p1, *sl 2 wyif, p2; rep from * to last 3 sts, sl 2 wyif, p1.
Row 13: With A, knit.
Row 14: With A, knit.
Row 15: With B, k1, sl 2 wyib, k2; rep from * to last 3 sts, sl 2 wyib, k1.
Row 16: With B, p1, *sl 2 wyif, p2; rep from * to last 3 sts, sl 2 wyif, p1.
[Rep Rows 1–16] twice.
Rep Rows 1–8.

Upper Border

With A, knit 5 rows.
With B, purl 3 rows.
With A, knit 4 rows.
Bind off, placing last st on crochet hook.

Edging

Sl st evenly spaced around the outside edge of dishcloth; join.
Finish off and weave in all ends. ●

Pistachio Nut Surprise

Skill Level
 EASY

Finished Size
Approx 10 inches square

Materials
- Lily Sugar 'n Cream medium weight cotton yarn (95 yds/57g per ball): 1 ball landscape #02244
- Size 7 (4.5mm) knitting needles or size required for gauge
- Size 6/G (4mm) crochet hook

4 MEDIUM

Gauge
16 sts = 4 inches/10cm in pat
To save time, take time to check gauge.

Pattern Note
Slip all sts as if to purl.

Instructions

Cast on 41 sts.
Purl 1 row.
Set up pat
Row 1 (RS): K5, *sl 1 wyib, k5; rep from * across.
Row 2: P5, *sl 1 wyif, p5; rep from * across.
Row 3: Rep Row 1.
Row 4: Purl.
[Rep Rows 1–4] 17 times.
Bind off, placing last st on crochet hook.

Edging
Ch 1, 3 sc in same corner, sc evenly spaced around outside of dishcloth, working 3 sc in each corner; join with sl st in first sc.
Finish off and weave in ends. ●

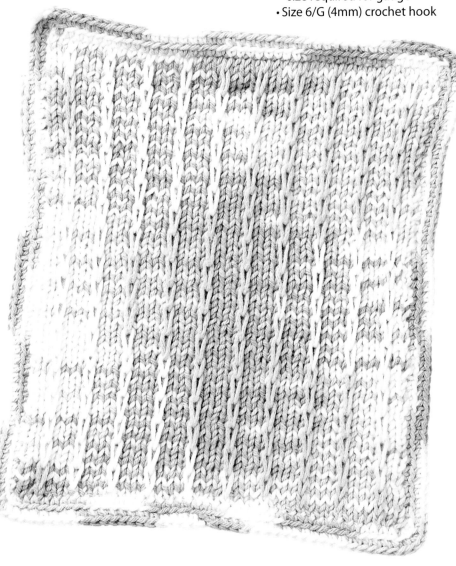

American School of Needlework • Berne, Indiana 46711 • DRGnetwork.com

Plum Jelly

Skill Level
 EASY

Finished Size
Approx 10 inches square

Materials
- Peaches & Crème medium weight cotton yarn (122 yds/71g per ball): 1 ball mauve #48
- Size 7 (4.5mm) knitting needles or size required for gauge
- Size 6/G (4mm) crochet hook

Gauge
16 sts = 4 inches/10cm in pat st
To save time, take time to check gauge.

Pattern Notes
Slip all sts as if to purl.
Pat includes sl sts alternating on each side of dominant vertical sts.

Instructions

Cast on 41 sts.
Row 1 (RS): *K4, sl 1 wyib; rep from * to last st, k1.
Row 2: P1, *sl 1 wyif, p4; rep from * across.
Row 3: K5, *sl 1 wyib, k4; rep from * to last st, k1.
Row 4: K5, *sl 1 wyif, k4; rep from * to last st, k1.
Row 5: K1, *sl 1 wyib, k4; rep from * across.
Row 6: *P4, sl 1 wyif; rep from * to last st, p1.
Row 7: K5, *sl 1 wyib, k4, rep from * to last st, k1.
Row 8: K5, *sl 1 wyif; k4, rep from * to last st, k1.
[Rep Rows 1–8] 8 times.
Bind off, placing last st on crochet hook.

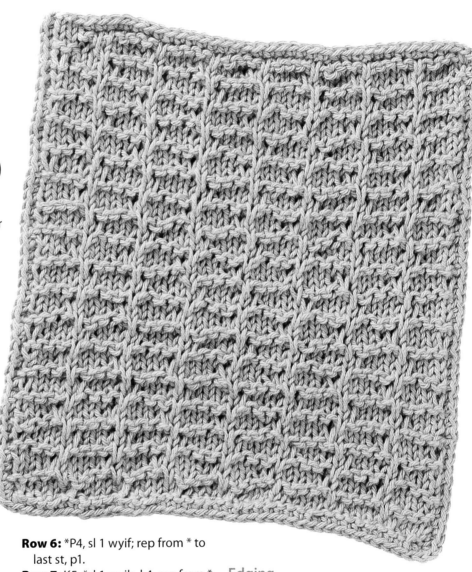

Edging
Ch 1, 3 sc in same corner, sc evenly spaced around the outside of the dishcloth, working 3 sc in each corner; join with sl st in first sc.
Finish off and weave in ends. ●

Tossed Salad

Skill Level
 EASY

Finished Size
Approx 10 inches square

Materials
- Peaches & Crème medium weight cotton yarn (98 yds/57g per ball): 1 ball shades of green #168 (A)
- Peaches & Crème medium weight cotton yarn (122 yds/71g per ball): 1 ball persimmon #33 (B)
- Size 7 (4.5mm) knitting needles or size required for gauge
- Size 6/G (4mm) crochet hook

Gauge
16 sts = 4 inches/10cm in pat
To save time, take time to check gauge.

Pattern Notes
Slip all sts as if to purl.
Carry color not in use loosely along edge.

Instructions

With A, cast on 40 sts.
Knit 1 row.
Set up pat
Row 1 (RS): With A, knit.
Row 2: Purl.
Row 3: With B, k4, *sl 2 wyib, k4; rep from * across.
Row 4: P4, *sl 2 wyif, p4; rep from * across.
Row 5: With A, knit.
Row 6: Purl.
Row 7: With B, k1, *sl 2 wyib, k4; rep from * to last 3 sts, sl 2 wyib, k1.
Row 8: P1, *sl 2 wyif, p4; rep from * to last 3 sts, sl 2 wyif, p1.
[Rep Rows 1–8] 7 times.
With A, knit 3 rows.
Bind off knitwise, placing last st on crochet hook.

Edging
With RS facing, ch 1, 3 sc in same corner, sc evenly spaced around the outside of dishcloth, working 3 sc in each corner; join with sl st in first sc.
Finish off and weave in all ends. ●

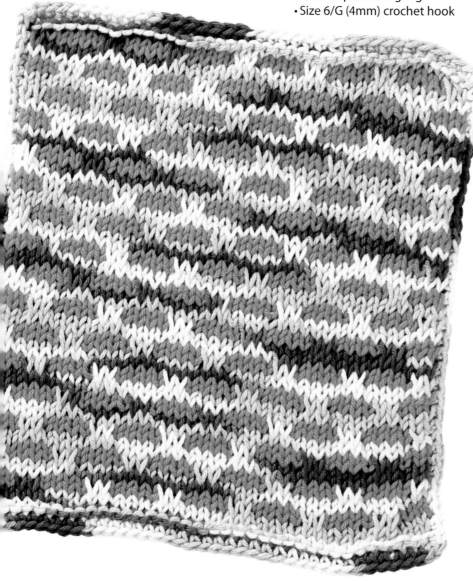

Blueberry Muffins

Skill Level
 EASY

Finished Size
Approx 10 inches square

Materials
• Lily Sugar 'n Cream medium weight cotton yarn (120 yds/71g per ball): 1 ball each hot blue #01742 (A) and white #00001 (B)
• Size 7 (4.5mm) knitting needles or size required for gauge
• Size 6/G (4mm) crochet hook

Gauge
18 sts = 4 inches/10cm in pat
To save time, take time to check gauge.

Pattern Notes
Slip all sts as if to purl.
Carry color not in use loosely along edge.

Instructions

Bottom Border
With A, cast on 45 sts.
Row 1 (WS): Purl.
Row 2 (RS): Knit.

Body
Row 1 (WS): With A, purl.
Row 2 (RS): With B, k1, sl 1 wyib, *k1, sl 3 wyib; rep from * to last 3 sts, k1, sl 1 wyib, k1.
Row 3: With B, k1,*p3, sl 1 wyif; rep from * to last 4 sts; p3, k1.
Row 4: With A, k2, *sl 1 wyib, k3; rep from * to last 3 sts; sl 1 wyib, k2.

Row 5: With A, purl.
Row 6: With B, k1, *sl 3 wyib, k1; rep from * across.
Row 7: With B, k1, p1, *sl 1 wyif, p3; rep from * to last 3 sts, sl 1 wyif, p1, k1.
Row 8: With A, k4, *sl 1 wyib, k3; rep from * to last st, k1.
[Rep Rows 1–8] 8 times.

Top Border
Next Row (WS): With A, purl.
Next Row (RS): With A, knit.
Bind off.

Edging
Rnd 1: Hold with RS facing and bound-off edge at top, with crochet hook, join B in upper right-hand corner, ch 1, 3 sc in same corner, sc evenly spaced around the outside of dishcloth, working 3 sc in each corner, join with sl st in first sc, changing to A.
Rnd 2: Ch 1, sc in each sc, working 3 sc in center sc of each corner; join in first sc.
Finish off and weave in all ends. ●

Blueberries & Cream

Skill Level

EASY

Finished Size
Approx 9½ inches square

Materials
- Lily Sugar 'n Cream worsted weight cotton yarn (95 yds/57g per ball): 1 ball Westport #02012
- Size 7 (4.5mm) knitting needles or size needed to obtain gauge
- Size 6/G (4mm) crochet hook

4 MEDIUM

Gauge
18 sts = 4 inches/10cm in pat
To save time, take time to check gauge.

Pattern Note
Slip all sts as if to purl.

Instructions

Cast on 46 sts.

Bottom Seed St Border
Row 1: *K1, p1; rep from * across.
Row 2: *P1, k1; rep from * across.
Rows 3 and 4: Rep Rows 1 and 2.
Row 5: Rep Row 1.

Set up Body pat
Note: Continue in Seed St Border pat as established over first and last 4 sts.
Row 1 (WS): [P1, K1] twice, k2, *p2, k2; rep from * to last 4 sts, [p1, k1] twice.
Row 2 (RS): [K1, p1] twice, p2, *sl 2 wyif, p2; rep from * to last 4 sts, [k1, p1] twice.
Rep Rows 1 and 2 of body pat until piece measures about 9 inches, ending by working a Row 1.

Top Seed St Border
Work same as Rows 1–5 of Bottom Seed St Border pat.
Bind off.
Weave in ends. ●

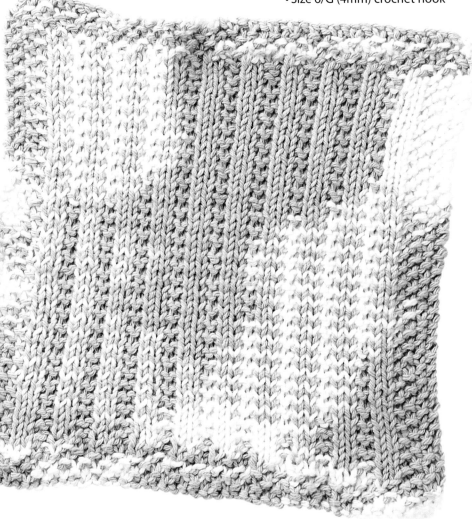

American School of Needlework • Berne, Indiana 46711 • DRGnetwork.com

Blue Ribbon Pastry

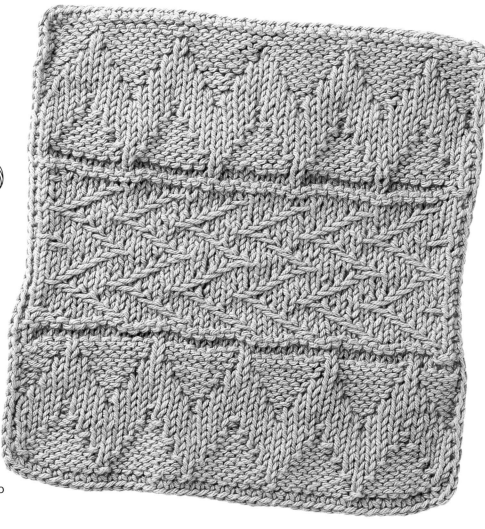

Skill Level
 EASY

Finished Size
Approx 10 inches square

Materials
• Peaches & Crème medium weight cotton yarn (122 yds/71g per ball): 1 ball light blue #26
• Size 7 (4.5mm) needles or size required for gauge
• Size 6/G (4mm) crochet hook

Gauge
17 sts = 4 inches/10cm in St st
To save time, take time to check gauge.

Instructions

Cast on 43 sts.
Knit 1 row.
Set up pat
Row 1 (RS): K2, *p7, k1; rep from * to last st, k1.
Row 2: K1, p1, *k7, p1; rep from * to last st, k1.
Row 3: K3, *p5, k3; rep from * across.
Row 4: K1, p2, *k5, p3; rep from * to last 8 sts, k5, p2, k1.
Row 5: K4, *p3, k5; rep from * to last 7 sts, p3, k4.
Row 6: K1, p3, *k3, p5; rep from * to last 7 sts, k3, p3, k1.
Row 7: K5, *p1, k7; rep from * to last 6 sts, p1, k5.
Row 8: K1, p4, *k1, p7; rep from * to last 6 sts, k1, p4, k1.
Row 9: K1, p1, *k7, p1; rep from * to last st, k1.

Row 10: K2, *p7, k1; rep from * to last st, k1.
Row 11: K1, p2, *k5, p3; rep from * to last 8 sts, k5, p2, k1.
Row 12: K3, *p5, k3; rep from * across.
Row 13: K1, p3, *k3, p5; rep from * to last 7 sts; k3, p3, k1.
Row 14: K4, *p3, k5; rep from * to last 7 sts, p3, k4.
Row 15: K1, p4, *k1, p7; rep from * to last 6 sts, k1, p4, k1.
Row 16: K5, *p1, k7; rep from * to last 6 sts, p1, k5.

Row 17: Knit.
Rows 18 and 19: K1, purl to last st, k1.
Row 20: K1, p19, p2tog, p20, k1. (42 sts)
Row 21: K2, *sl 2 wyif, k4; rep from * to last 4 sts; sl 2 wyif, k2.
Row 22: K1, sl 2 wyib, *p4, sl 2 wyib; rep from * to last 3 sts, p2, k1.
Row 23: K4, *sl 2 wyif, k4; rep from * to last 2 sts, k2.
Row 24: K1, p4, *sl 2 wyib, p4; rep from * to last st, k1.

Row 25: K6, *sl 2 wyif, k4; rep from * across.

Row 26: K1, p2, *sl 2 wyib, p4; rep from * to last 3 sts, sl 1 wyib, p1, k1.

Row 27: K2, *sl 2 wyif, k4; rep from * to last 4 sts, sl 2 wyif, k2.

Row 28: K1, p2, *sl 2 wyib, p4; rep from * to last 3 sts, sl 1 wyib, p1, k1.

Row 29: K6, *sl 2 wyif, k4; rep from * across.

Row 30: K1, p4, *sl 2 wyib, p4; rep from * to last st, k1.

Row 31: K4, *sl 2 wyif, k4; rep from * to last 2 sts, k2.

Row 32: K1, p1, sl 1 wyib, *p4, sl 2 wyib; rep from * to last 3 sts, p2, k1.

Rep Rows 21–32.

Knit 3 rows.

Next row: K1, p19, inc, p20, k1. (43 sts)

Work Rows 1–16.

Next row: K1, purl to last st, k1. Bind off, placing last st on crochet hook.

Edging

Ch 1, 3 sc in same corner, sc evenly spaced around the outside of dishcloth, working 3 sc in each corner, join with sl st in first sc. Finish off and weave in ends. ●

General Information

Knit Abbreviations & Symbols

approx	approximately
beg	begin/beginning
CC	contrasting color
ch	chain stitch
cm	centimeter(s)
cn	cable needle
dec	decrease/decreases/decreasing
dpn(s)	double-pointed needle(s)
g	gram
inc	increase/increases/increasing
k	knit
k2tog	knit 2 stitches together
LH	left hand
lp(s)	loop(s)
m	meter(s)
M1	make one stitch
MC	main color
mm	millimeter(s)
oz	ounce(s)
p	purl

pat(s)	pattern(s)
p2tog	purl 2 stitches together
psso	pass slipped stitch over
p2sso	pass 2 slipped stitches over
rem	remain/remaining
rep	repeat(s)
rev St st	reverse stockinette stitch
RH	right hand
rnd(s)	rounds
RS	right side
skp	slip, knit, pass stitch over—one stitch decreased
sk2p	slip 1, knit 2 together, pass slip stitch over, then knit 2 together—2 stitches have been decreased
sl	slip
sl 1k	slip 1 knitwise
sl 1p	slip 1 purlwise
sl st	slip stitch(es)
ssk	slip, slip, knit these 2 stitches together—a decrease

st(s)	stitch(es)
St st	stockinette stitch/stocking stitch
tbl	through back loop(s)
tog	together
WS	wrong side
wyib	with yarn in back
wyif	with yarn in front
yd(s)	yard(s)
yfwd	yarn forward
yo	yarn over

[] work instructions within brackets as many times as directed

() work instructions within parentheses in the place directed

** repeat instructions following the asterisks as directed

* repeat instructions following the single asterisk as directed

" inch(es)

Standard Yarn Weight System
Categories of yarn, gauge ranges, and recommended needle sizes

Yarn Weight Symbol & Category Names	1 SUPER FINE	2 FINE	3 LIGHT	4 MEDIUM	5 BULKY	6 SUPER BULKY
Type of Yarns in Category	Sock, Fingering, Baby	Sport, Baby	DK, Light Worsted	Worsted, Afghan, Aran	Chunky, Craft, Rug	Bulky, Roving
Knit Gauge Range* in Stockinette Stitch to 4 inches	27–32 sts	23–26 sts	21–24 sts	16–20 sts	12–15 sts	6–11 sts
Recommended Needle in Metric Size Range	2.25–3.25mm	3.25–3.75mm	3.75–4.5mm	4.5–5.5mm	5.5–8mm	8mm and larger
Recommended Needle U.S. Size Range	1 to 3	3 to 5	5 to 7	7 to 9	9 to 11	11 and larger

* **GUIDELINES ONLY:** The above reflect the most commonly used gauges and needle sizes for specific yarn categories.

Crochet Stitches

Single Crochet (sc)

Insert the hook in the second chain through the center of the V. Bring the yarn over the hook from back to front.

Draw the yarn through the chain stitch and onto the hook.

Again bring yarn over the hook from back to front and draw it through both loops on hook.

For additional rows of single crochet, insert the hook under both loops of the previous stitch instead of through the center of the V as when working into the chain stitch.

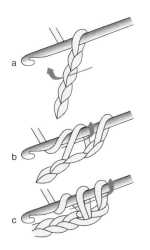

Slip Stitch (sl st)

Insert hook under both loops of the stitch, bring yarn over the hook from back to front and draw it through the stitch and the loop on the hook.

How to Check Gauge

A correct stitch gauge is very important. Please take the time to work a stitch gauge swatch about 4 x 4 inches. Measure the swatch. If the number of stitches and rows are fewer than indicated under "Gauge" in the pattern, your needles are too large. Try another swatch with smaller-size needles. If the number of stitches and rows are more than indicated under "Gauge" in the pattern, your needles are too small. Try another swatch with larger-size needles.

Inches Into Millimeters & Centimeters

All measurements are rounded off slightly.

inches	mm	cm	inches	cm	inches	cm	inches	cm
⅛	3	0.3	5	12.5	21	53.5	38	96.5
¼	6	0.6	5½	14	22	56.0	39	99.0
⅜	10	1.0	6	15.0	23	58.5	40	101.5
½	13	1.3	7	18.0	24	61.0	41	104.0
⅝	15	1.5	8	20.5	25	63.5	42	106.5
¾	20	2.0	9	23.0	26	66.0	43	109.0
⅞	22	2.2	10	25.5	27	68.5	44	112.0
1	25	2.5	11	28.0	28	71.0	45	114.5
1¼	32	3.8	12	30.5	29	73.5	46	117.0
1½	38	3.8	13	33.0	30	76.0	47	119.5
1¾	45	4.5	14	35.5	31	79.0	48	122.0
2	50	5.0	15	38.0	32	81.5	49	124.5
2½	65	6.5	16	40.5	33	84.0	50	127.0
3	75	7.5	17	43.0	34	86.5		
3½	90	9.0	18	46.0	35	89.0		
4	100	10.0	19	48.5	36	91.5		
4½	115	11.5	20	51.0	37	94.0		

Knitting Needle Conversion Chart

U.S.	1	2	3	4	5	6	7	8	9	10	10½	11	13	15	17	19	35	50
Continental-mm	2.25	2.75	3.25	3.5	3.75	4	4.5	5	5.5	6	6.5	8	9	10	12.75	15	19	25

Skill Levels

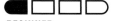

BEGINNER
Beginner projects for first-time knitters using basic stitches. Minimal shaping.

EASY
Easy projects using basic stitches, repetitive stitch patterns, simple color changes and simple shaping and finishing.

INTERMEDIATE
Intermediate projects with a variety of stitches, mid-level shaping and finishing.

EXPERIENCED
Experienced projects using advanced techniques and stitches, detailed shaping and refined finishing.

American School of Needlework ®
excellence in instruction

TOLL-FREE ORDER LINE or to request a free catalog (800) 582-6643
Customer Service (800) 282-6643, **Fax** (800) 882-6643
Visit DRGnetwork.com.

We have made every effort to ensure the accuracy and completeness of these instructions.
We cannot, however, be responsible for human error, typographical mistakes or variations in individual work.

ISBN: 978-1-59012-206-8   All rights reserved.   Printed in USA   4 5 6 7 8 9